At a Glance™ Series

DVD and

DVD Metal Guitar

Written by Joe Charupakorn, Kurt Plahna, Mike Mueller & Chad Johnson
Video Performers: Troy Stetina & Marcus Henderson

ISBN: 978-1-4234-6225-5

HAL•LEONARD® CORPORATION
7777 W. BLUEMOUND RD. P.O. BOX 13819 MILWAUKEE, WI 53213

Visit Hal Leonard Online at
www.halleonard.com

Table of Contents

Introduction

Welcome to *DVD Metal Guitar*, from Hal Leonard's exciting At a Glance series. Not as in-depth and slow moving as traditional method books, the material in *DVD Metal Guitar* is presented in a snappy and fun manner intended to have you headbanging in virtually no time at all. Plus, the At a Glance series uses real riffs and licks by real artists to illustrate how the concepts you're learning are applied in metal's greatest moments. For example, in *DVD Metal Guitar*, you'll learn the riffs to such classics as Ozzy Osbourne's "Bark at the Moon," Iron Maiden's "The Trooper," and System of a Down's "Chop Suey," to name just a few.

Additionally, each book in the At a Glance series comes with a DVD containing video lessons that correspond to the printed material. In these videos, ace instructors Marcus Henderson and Troy Stetina will show you in great detail everything from how to palm mute power chords to detuning your guitar straight to the depths of hell. As you work through *DVD Metal Guitar*, try to play the examples first on your own, and then check out the DVD for additional help or to see if you played them correctly. As the saying goes, "A picture is worth a thousand words," so be sure to use this invaluable tool on your quest to becoming a master metal guitar player.

METAL RHYTHM GUITAR

In addition to crucifixes, headless bats, and the number 666, heavy metal is famous for its powerful rhythm guitar riffs. These rhythm guitar parts have formed the backbone for immortal metal anthems. From power chords to single-note riffs, chromatic chord movement to the all-important palm mute, we're going to cover it all.

Power Chords

The foundation of metal rhythm guitar is the **power chord**, and many timeless riffs have been constructed using nothing more. Power chords are so essential to the genre that if you couldn't play anything else, you'd still be able to rock hard enough to get some groupies!

The reason power chords are so popular is A) they sound powerful (pun intended), and B) they're easy to play. Here are two common ways to play a power chord:

Two-String Shape

This is played starting with the index finger on either the low E or A string (or less commonly starting on the D string) and the ring finger on the next higher string, two frets away. The pinky can also be used instead of the ring finger if it's too hard to stretch. The root (or name) of the chord is derived from the note played on the lowest string. Below is an A5 chord, named as such because the lowest note of the chord is the fifth fret of the low E string, which is an A note.

Watch what Guns N' Roses does with the two-string power chord. This riff is tricky, so definitely take it slow at first.

"WELCOME TO THE JUNGLE"
Guns N' Roses

Words and Music by W. Axl Rose, Slash, Izzy Stradlin',
Duff McKagan and Steven Adler

Three-String Shape

This is based on the two-string power chord but has the root doubled an octave higher. Adding the higher note gives the chord an extra boost of chunkiness. Here's the A5 power chord again with the added octave.

Check out how the Scorpions use this basic shape by moving it around with a catchy rhythm in the intro to "Rock You like a Hurricane."

Words and Music by Herman Rarebell,
Klaus Meine and Rudolf Schenker

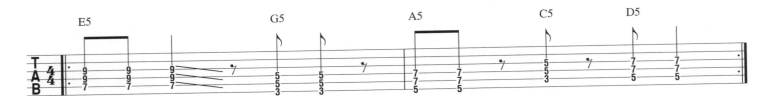

Generally speaking, you might tend toward the three-string shape when you want a big, sustained sound, while the two-string shape may work better for more active riffs where you're sliding around or moving between chords quickly. It's generally easier to move the two-string shape around, so if a riff is really fast, stick with that.

 Let's take a look at some typical power chord riffs. Here's one in the key of E minor with the two-string shape. This one moves around a little bit, so if you're new to power chords, practice just changing from chord to chord first before trying to play the riff in rhythm.

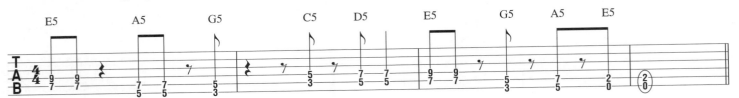

 And here's another one, this time in A minor and using the three-string shape. Try for a con-nected, "wall-of-sound" feel on this one.

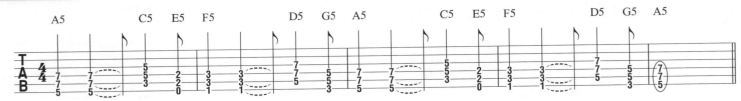

Palm Muting

Now these power chord riffs can be made much more "metal" with various techniques, and by far one of the most common is **palm muting**. This adds a chunky sound to chords and also helps to keep the guitar under control, which is important if you've got a lot of gain on the amp.

 To get the palm-muted sound, just position your pick hand so that your palm lightly presses against the string near the bridge. Don't push down too hard though. The farther you move in from the bridge, the more muted the sound becomes. Check it out both ways on the DVD. Each way is equally valid; it just depends on what type of sound you're trying to get.

You can apply the palm-muting technique to just about any power chord riff.

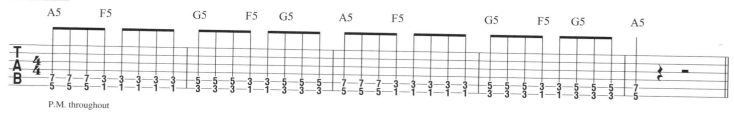

P.M. throughout

The verse of "Rock You like a Hurricane" also features power chords in a steady eighth-note rhythm with a palm mute applied throughout.

"ROCK YOU LIKE A HURRICANE"
Scorpions

Words and Music by Herman Rarebell,
Klaus Meine and Rudolf Schenker

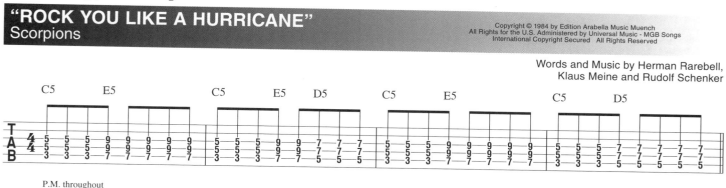

P.M. throughout

You can also use palm muting with open-position chords. For example, Van Halen applied palm muting to great effect in the intro to "Ain't Talkin' 'Bout Love" using the Am, F, and G chord shapes. The palm mute is used to keep the notes clearly separated.

"AIN'T TALKIN' 'BOUT LOVE"
Van Halen

Words and Music by David Lee Roth, Edward Van Halen,
Alex Van Halen and Michael Anthony

*Tune down 1/2 step:
(low to high) E♭-A♭-D♭-G♭-B♭-E♭

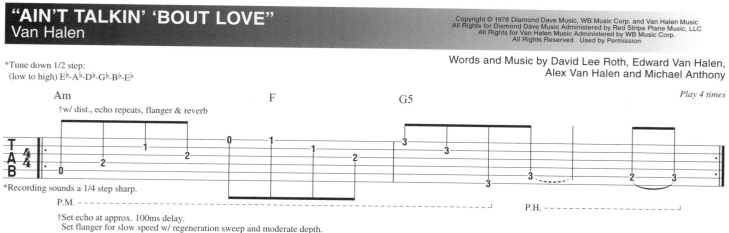

*Recording sounds a 1/4 step sharp.

†Set echo at approx. 100ms delay.
  Set flanger for slow speed w/ regeneration sweep and moderate depth.

Pedal Tone Riffs

One of the most common devices used in conjunction with palm muting is the **pedal tone riff**. In these riffs, you repeat a palm-muted bass note, usually an open string, and release the mute for a few power chords on top.

For instance, if you're playing in E minor, you might mute the low E string in between power chords. If you're in A minor, you might mute the open A string in between chords. You hear this kind of thing all the time. Developing the coordination will take a bit of practice, but with time, you'll instinctively know when to mute and when to let things ring.

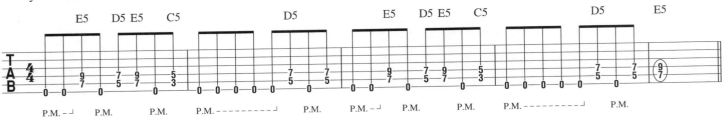

Van Halen's "Panama" also uses an E pedal tone, but this time it's played on the seventh fret of the A string. Add the palm muting technique you just learned to these pedal tones.

"PANAMA"
Van Halen

Words and Music by David Lee Roth, Edward Van Halen,
Alex Van Halen and Michael Anthony

Tune down 1/2 step:
(low to high) E♭-A♭-D♭-G♭-B♭-E♭

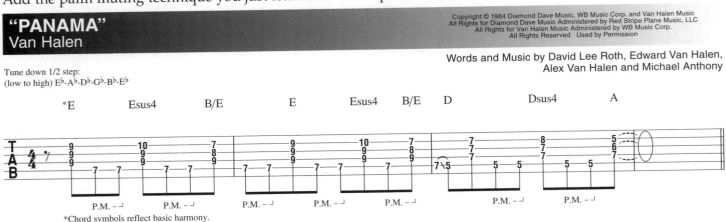

*Chord symbols reflect basic harmony.

A common trick is to mix in some sixteenth notes on the pedal tone. Watch the DVD to get the rhythm and feel of this riff right.

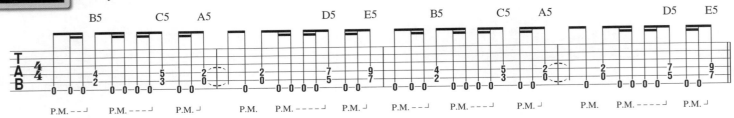

Here's the fretboard-melting riff from Ozzy Osbourne's "Bark at the Moon." The sixteenth-note A pedal tones must be played very precisely, especially at this fast tempo. Also note that the first chord is a three-string power chord played on the D, G, and B strings. When a three-string power chord is played on this string set, the pinky moves up a fret from the shape you learned earlier.

"BARK AT THE MOON"
Ozzy Osbourne

Words and Music by
Ozzy Osbourne

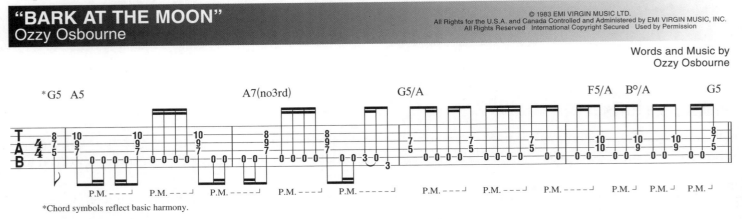

*Chord symbols reflect basic harmony.

Inverted Power Chords and Other Dyads

When you **invert** a two-note power chord, which is a 5th, you get a 4th. For example, these chords:

Could also be played like this:

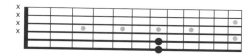

All we're doing is moving one of the notes either up or down an octave. In this E5, for instance, we can move the E up an octave or the B down an octave, like this:

The inverted power chords can be played pretty easily using one finger. When you mix these inverted power chords with the use of slides, hammer-ons, or pull-offs, you can get some great sounding riffs. Eddie Van Halen was a master at this type of thing.

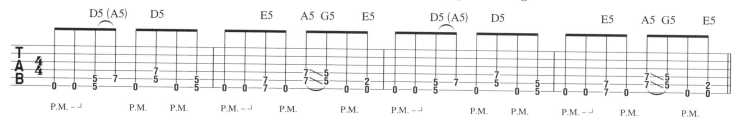

One of the all-time, classic, must-know riffs is "Smoke on the Water." The intro riff is comprised of easy-to-play, one-finger, 4th dyads.

"SMOKE ON THE WATER"
Deep Purple

Words and Music by Ritchie Blackmore, Ian Gillan,
Roger Glover, Jon Lord and Ian Paice

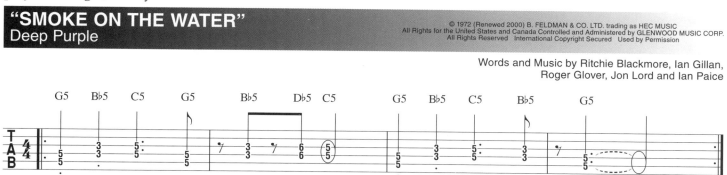

The intro riff to "Heaven Tonight" shows how Swedish shred king Yngwie J. Malmsteen uses a 4th dyad in conjunction with a low E pedal tone.

"HEAVEN TONIGHT"
Yngwie Malmsteen

Words and Music by Yngwie Malmsteen
and Joe Lynn Turner

Tune down 1/2 step:
(low to high) E♭-A♭-D♭-G♭-B♭-E♭

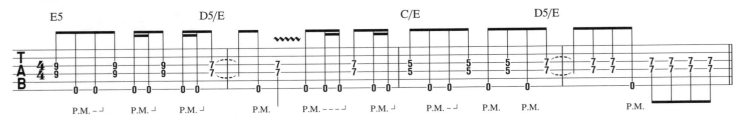

 Here's another one in A minor. You might have to try this one slow at first to catch all the subtleties (pull-offs, slides, etc.).

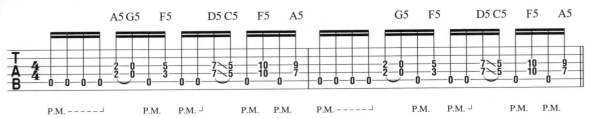

 And you're not just limited to 4ths and 5ths either. Other dyads are used as well, like:

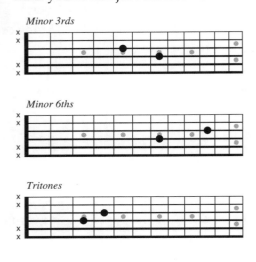

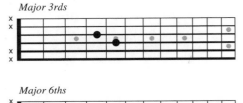

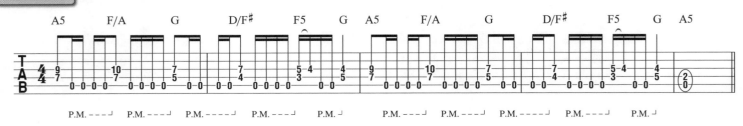 You can get some pretty colorful rhythms by using these dyads. You might come up with something like this:

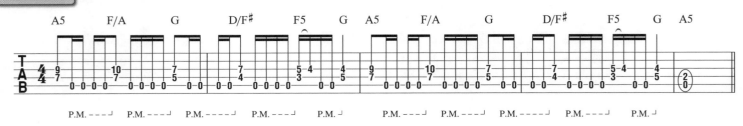

The intro riff to Def Leppard's "Photograph" uses 4ths, 3rds, and 5ths.

"PHOTOGRAPH"
Def Leppard

Words and Music by Joe Elliott, Steve Clark, Peter Willis,
Richard Savage, Richard Allen and R.J. Lange

Tune down 1/2 step:
(low to high) E♭-A♭-D♭-G♭-B♭-E♭

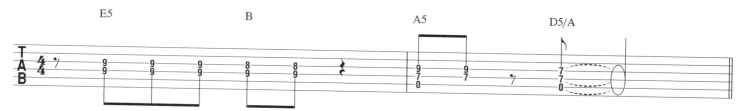

Adding Single Notes

Besides dyads, **single notes** are often used in metal rhythm parts. You can combine them with a power-chord riff, like Yngwie Malmsteen might do. All we're doing there is adding notes from the E minor scale.

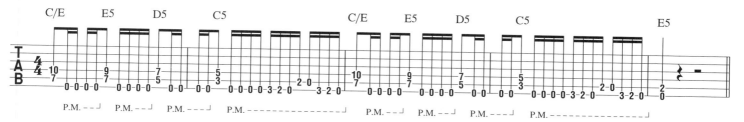

Check out what Yngwie Malmsteen did in "I'll See the Light Tonight." Here he uses minor 6th and perfect 5th dyads against an open A pedal. At the end of the phrase, he adds a fill from the A natural minor scale and later adds a spooky diminished-based tritone single note riff.

"I'LL SEE THE LIGHT TONIGHT"
Yngwie Malmsteen

Words and Music by Yngwie Malmsteen
and Jeff Scott Soto

Tune down 1/2 step:
(low to high) E♭-A♭-D♭-G♭-B♭-E♭

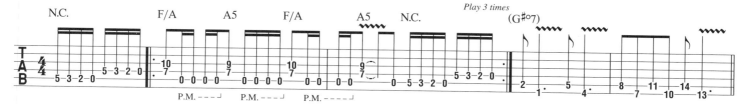

You can also create a riff using nothing but single notes. The minor pentatonic and blues scale are common scales to use for these types of riffs. This approach works great with songs that are in the slower to medium tempo range. You'll hear bands like Tesla, Metallica, or Black Sabbath do this.

Here's an E minor pentatonic example. Make sure you don't rush the slide.

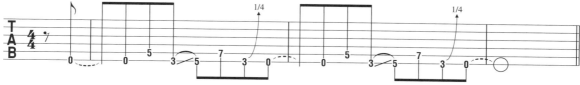

Here's one from the E blues scale. This one has might be tricky, so try it slow at first.

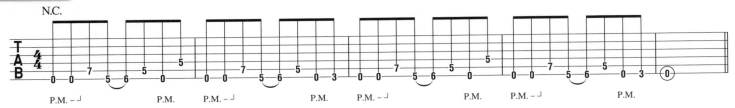

Check out how UFO creates a catchy E minor riff using exclusively single notes.

"ROCK BOTTOM"
UFO

Words and Music by Phillip John Mogg
and Michael Schenker

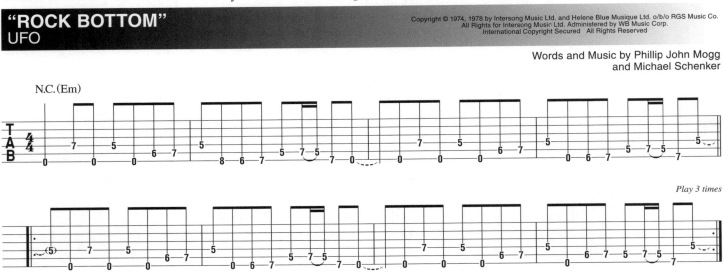

Or let's not forget Aerosmiths' metal-meets-boogie classic "Walk this Way."

"WALK THIS WAY"
Aerosmith

Words and Music by Steven Tyler
and Joe Perry

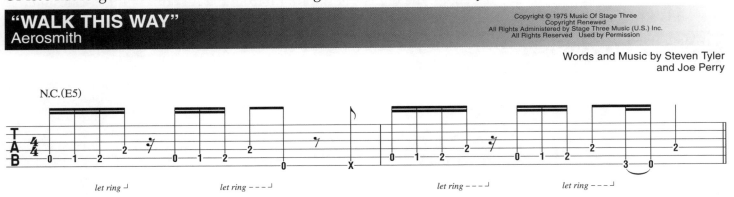

Chromatic or Non-Diatonic Notes

Finally, for really wicked-sounding riffs, **non-diatonic** notes are often used. This means using notes that are not part of the key—kind of like putting black pepper on someone's vanilla ice cream. This is the best way to add a touch of "evil" to your riffs.

The ♭2nd and ♭5th are really common choices in this realm, as they are especially eerie-sounding and dissonant, but any note can do as long as it sounds "off" from the key—try a riff using major 7ths maybe. You can interject these tones as single notes or build power chords from them.

You've heard Metallica make use of this device quite often.

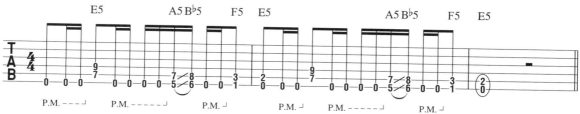

Or something like this, which is full of sinister half steps.

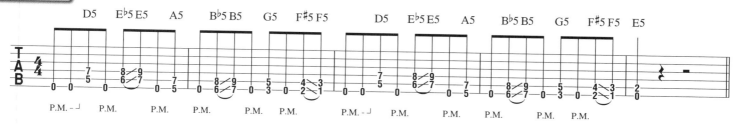

Check out Testament's "Practice What You Preach" for more evil ♭5ths and ♭2nds.

"PRACTICE WHAT YOU PREACH"
Testament

Words and Music by Eric Peterson, Luciano Clemente,
Alex Skolnick, Gregory Christian and Charles Billy

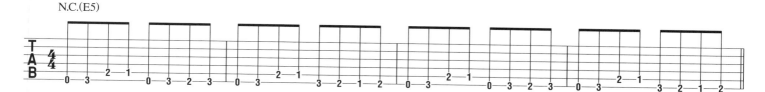

To sum it up, the main elements of metal rhythm guitar are power chords, palm muting, pedal-tone riffs, other dyads, single notes, and chromatic tones. And one more thing—you have to play with attitude!

METAL LICKS

From the first guttural strains of Black Sabbath to the new wave of British heavy metal to hair metal and Nu metal and every metal in between, the guitar has always been the driving force behind the genre's punishing sound.

Now that you've got a handle on the rhythm guitar side of things, let's check out where the action is: metal lead guitar. We're going to look at the greatest metal licks of all time, from ten of the genre's legendary practitioners.

Black Sabbath

Heavy metal was born out of the blues. And though guitarists like Eric Clapton and Jimmy Page had established the blues-rock sound in the sixties, it was Black Sabbath's Tony Iommi that first plunged those blues licks into the deepest pits of hell. Metal has never been the same since.

Iommi based his licks on the minor pentatonic and blues scales. This Iommi-style lick comes from the E minor pentatonic scale. Note the use of 1½ step overbends to place added emphasis on the minor tonality.

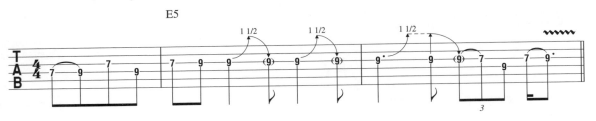

"Paranoid" is a classic Iommi "must-know" riff; it's practically a rite of passage for all metal guitarists.

"PARANOID"
Black Sabbath

Words and Music by Anthony Iommi, John Osbourne,
William Ward and Terence Butler

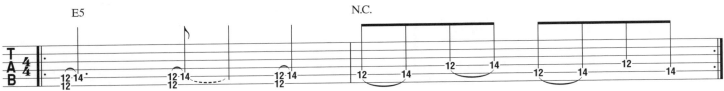

Kiss

While Black Sabbath was crafting the *soundtrack* to Hell, proto-glam metallers Kiss were busy designing the netherworld's wardrobe. Kiss not only had the flashiest outfits, they also had the most explosive live shows, with more pyrotechnics than the Macy's Fourth of July spectacle.

Like Iommi, Kiss guitarist Ace Frehley based his metal licks primarily on the minor pentatonic scale, even invoking the great Chuck Berry in his solo on "Rock and Roll All Nite." This next lick, based on the A minor pentatonic scale, is an ode to Spaceman Ace. A repeating lick like this is good for building up sparks in a solo.

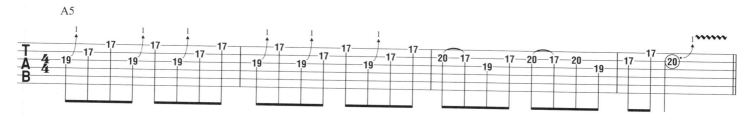

Here's another repeating lick from the outro to "Deuce." This is similar to the lick we just checked out.

Words and Music by
Gene Simmons

Tune down 1/2 step:
(low to high) E♭-A♭-D♭-G♭-B♭-E♭

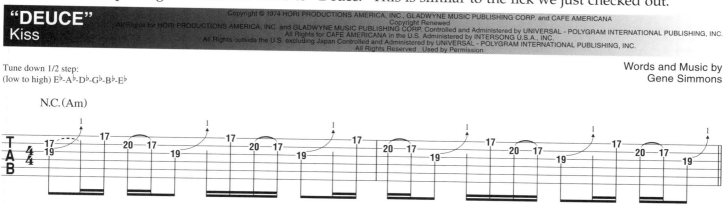

Judas Priest

By the late seventies, a new wave of heavy metal was brewing over in the U.K. That movement's first export, Judas Priest, with guitarists Glenn Tipton and K.K. Downing (outfitted with spikey leatherwear), pushed blues-based metal harder than ever before.

Our next lick is inspired by Tipton's solo in "You've Got Another Thing Comin'." It's based on the F♯ blues scale and uses some bluesy quarter-step bends on the ♭3rd for added dynamic. Be sure to add some tasty vibrato to that last note.

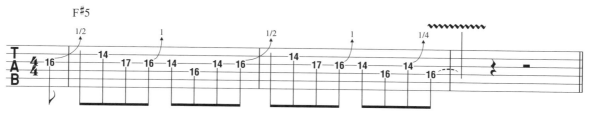

Here's more F♯ blues scale madness that may make you want to break the law!

Words and Music by Glenn Tipton,
Rob Halford and K.K. Downing

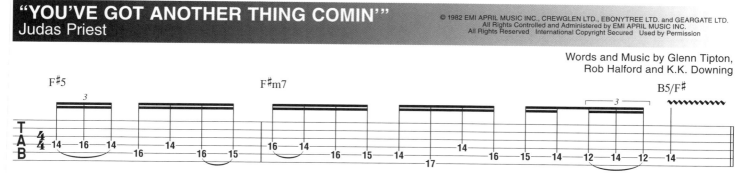

Iron Maiden

Around that same time, another UK metal act, Iron Maiden, was crafting their own killer sound, setting the new standard for two-guitar metal bands—a mark that to this day is still the most revered in the genre. Maiden's twin-guitar lead harmonies are an unmistakable signature, and this approach has been widely imitated throughout metal history.

 This lick comes courtesy of the bluesier Adrian Smith. With syncopated full-step bends providing the drama, this lick is culled from the E minor pentatonic scale and contains bends on the higher frets of each of the top three strings in the E minor pentatonic box.

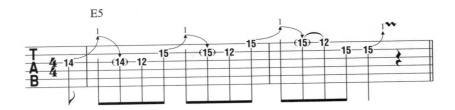

The other half of Iron Maiden's two-axe attack, Dave Murray, also wields a mighty blues hand, but can shred diatonically equally as well, providing a good contrast.

 This lick, similar to the one he played in "The Trooper," is set in E minor and requires a slight pinky stretch. Try not to rush the pull-offs.

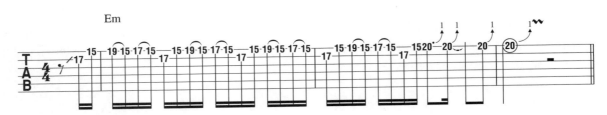

The solo in "The Trooper" features both bluesy bends and diatonic shred in harmonized glory.

"THE TROOPER"
Iron Maiden

Words and Music by
Steven Harris

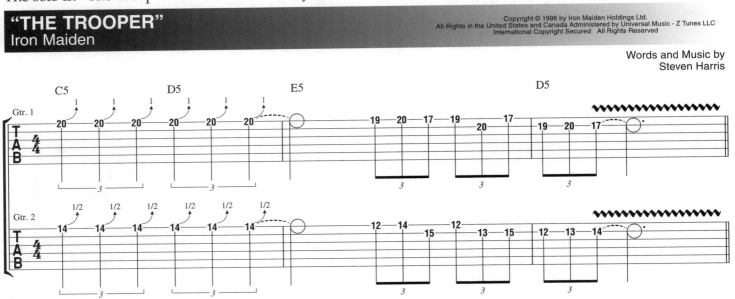

Metallica

In the early eighties, an explosive young band called Metallica emerged from San Francisco, combining heavy metal with the breakneck pace of punk in a new music form called thrash.

With riff-meister James Hetfield providing the backdrop, lead guitarist Kirk Hammett combined speed picking, legato techniques, scale sequencing, and whammy bar maneuvers to create a whole new lead guitar style in metal.

The following lick is built on a descending sequence of eighth-note triplets, much like Hammett uses in "Fade to Black." This lick requires a bit of alternate-picking precision, so a metronome might prove very helpful here. Start off at a slow tempo and make sure your triplets are clean and evenly spaced (three notes to a beat).

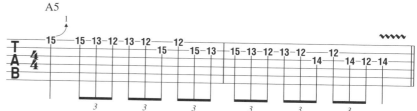

Spanish Phrygian Mode: 1–♭2–3–4–5–♭6–♭7

Later in the band's career, Kirk Hammett began to experiment with new sounds and techniques, such as the wah pedal and exotic scales. One such scale was the E Spanish Phrygian mode, which is the fifth mode of A harmonic minor. It's just like a natural minor scale, except that instead of a flatted 3rd degree, it contains a flatted 2nd. This tapping lick, similar to Hammett's in "Wherever I May Roam," makes fabulous use of that ♭2nd to major 3rd rub. Make sure to time the tap just right, otherwise it will sound sloppy.

This type of exotic, middle-eastern sound is favored by modern-day shredders, who may have initially picked it up from Yngwie Malmsteen's use of harmonic minor scales.

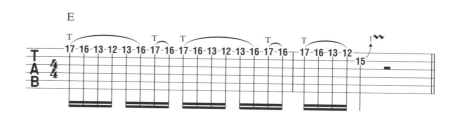

Hammet always liked to push the envelope with exotic sounds. In his solo on "Breadfan," he takes a repeating shape based on a third-inversion major 7 chord and moves it up chromatically, creating a jazzy "out" sound not common in metal. By the way, don't worry about all this theory talk. Hammet probably didn't know the technical name of what he was playing. He's got good ears and just hears these dissonant licks.

"BREADFAN"
Metallica

Words and Music by Anthony Bourge,
John Burke Shelley and Raymond Phillips

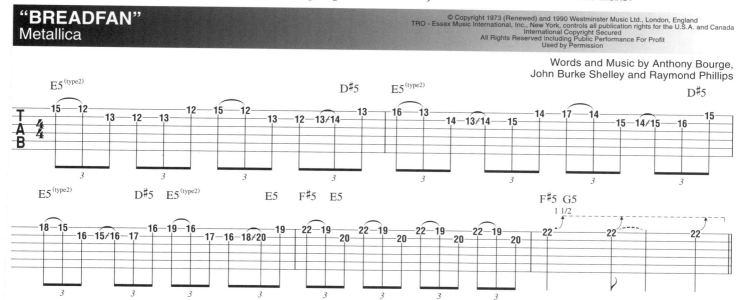

Megadeth

Megadeth founder and guitarist Dave Mustaine was actually an original member of Metallica. Lucky for us metal fans, it didn't work out, and instead we got two legendary thrash bands out of the deal.

This next lick is inspired by Mustaine's use of a repeated pull-off motif in E minor, from his classic "Holy Wars… The Punishment Due," (*Rust in Peace*). It has a similar shape to the Dave Murray lick we looked at earlier, but the ♭5 note on fret 15 of the B string gives the lick a bluesier vibe.

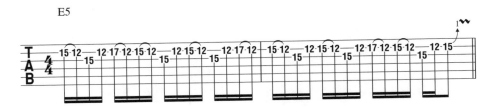

Mustaine's sense of rhythm is impeccable. Make sure not to rush the lick, as is easy to do. Check out the slow version on the DVD to get the timing right.

On "Crush 'Em," Megadeth pulverizes us with some fiery G minor pentatonic shred.

"CRUSH 'EM"
Megadeth

Words and Music by Dave Mustaine,
Marty Friedman and Bud Prager

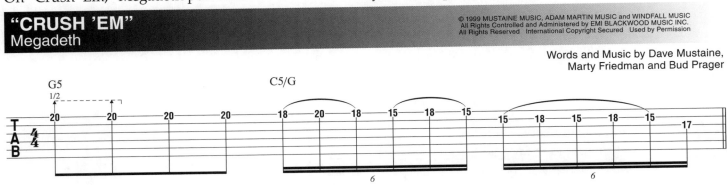

Scorpions

Sporting black and white Gibson Flying Vs and Explorers, respectively, Scorpions guitarists Rudy Schenker and Mattias Jabs rocked the minor scale like no one else. That being said, Jabs would occasionally insert chromatic passing tones into his lines—a great tool when you want to use a speedy passage to get from one target note to another without sounding like a scale exercise.

Here's an example of that technique, inspired by a similar run in the solo to "Rock You Like a Hurricane." It's a good, strong lick to use as a climax to a solo. Be sure to use alternate picking for a steady rhythm and add vibrato to milk out the last note.

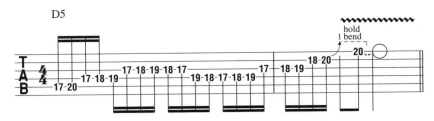

In the intro solo of "Rock you Like a Hurricane," Jabs whips out a blazing E blues scale run played as an alternate-picked sextuplet at a tempo of 124 beats per minute. Think you have the chops to pull it off?

"ROCK YOU LIKE A HURRICANE"
Scorpions

Words and Music by Herman Rarebell,
Klaus Meine and Rudolf Schenker

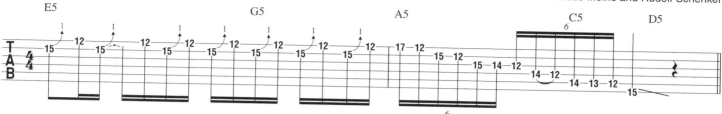

Randy Rhoads

Schooled equally in the blues and classical music, Ozzy Osbourne guitarist Randy Rhoads rewrote the book on metal guitar phrasing and technique. His all too brief career (ended by a tragic plane crash) helped shape the sound of generations of metal guitarists that followed.

One of his undervalued contributions was his use of sequences and motifs, something derived from his classical studies. Our next lick, similar to one Randy played in "I Don't Know," takes a four-note sequence down the fretboard in half-step increments for an "out" sounding lick that lands comfortably on the 3rd, B. The reason he can get away with all of these notes that are not in key is that the last note, which is prominently held, resolves perfectly in key. For authenticity, play the lick like Randy did and use a slight palm mute on this lick.

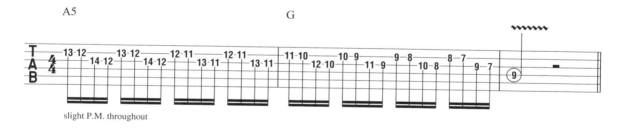

Here's a blistering sequence from Randy's solo on "Flying High Again." Accent (hit harder) the first note of each beat.

"FLYING HIGH AGAIN"
Ozzy Osbourne

Words and Music by Ozzy Osbourne, Randy Rhoads,
Bob Daisley and Lee Kerslake

Tune down 1/2 step:
(low to high) E♭-A♭-D♭-G♭-B♭-E♭

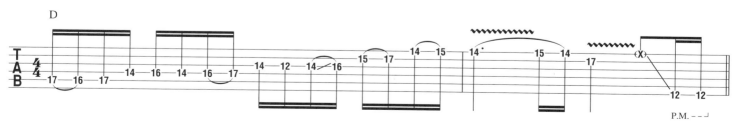

Zakk Wylde

After Randy's tragic passing in 1982, Ozzy went through several capable guitarists, including Brad Gillis and Jake E. Lee, but none who seemed to fit the mold—until Zakk Wylde, that is. With monster chops to match his monster physique and an unmistakable bullseye guitar, Wylde has become arguably his generation's biggest guitar hero.

Like Rhoads before him, Wylde is also fond of sequencing, particularly using the minor pentatonic scale. Here is one of Zakk's favorite pentatonic licks. This lick will help you learn your moveable A minor pentatonic shapes up on the top two strings.

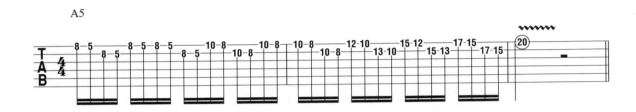

Here's a sequence in a similar vein from "No More Tears." Here he blazes through several two-string shapes mostly derived from D minor pentatonic. Be sure to use strict alternate picking for the first three measures—ouch!

"NO MORE TEARS"
Ozzy Osbourne

Words and Music by Ozzy Osbourne, Zakk Wylde,
Randy Castillo, Michael Inez and John Purdell

Drop D tuning down 1/2 step:
(low to high) D♭-A♭-D♭-G♭-B♭-E♭

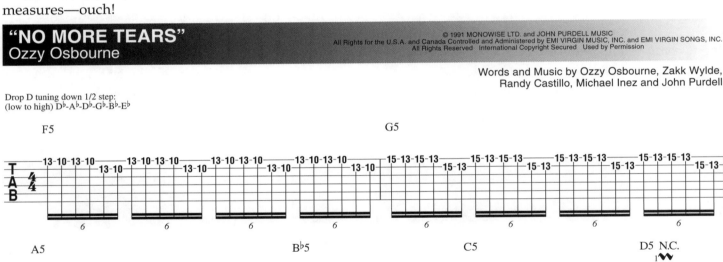

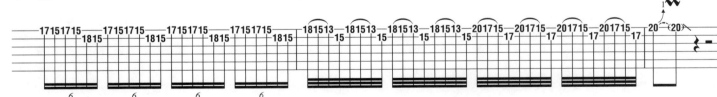

Dimebag Darrell

The nineties were a dark time for metal fans, as an anti-guitar hero sentiment sadly caught hold. Guitarists that finally came up for air after shredding their lives away in the practice room were met with an unpleasant surprise. Rather than being greeted with the expected hero's welcome, considering the hours of metronome-aided diminished arpeggios, they were instead shunned like lepers. But one band, Pantera, ripped through that dark curtain like a razor.

Pantera guitarist Darrell Abbott, better known as Dimebag, took his cue largely from Eddie Van Halen, combining supersonic blues-scale runs with legato techniques and even his very own signature scale pattern all played through solid-state amps. But to best sum up Dimebag's playing, the man could flat-out shred the blues scale.

This lick, similar to ones Dime played in "Cowboys from Hell" and "Walk," is built on a six-note E blues-scale sequence. This will get you into sextuplet-mode fast!

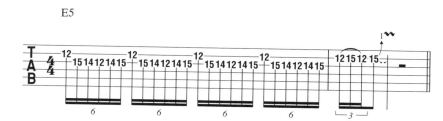

Besides being able to shred the blues scale, Dimebag could also play diatonically when it was called for.

"PLANET CARAVAN"
Pantera

Words and Music by Frank Iommi, John Osbourne,
William Ward and Terence Butler

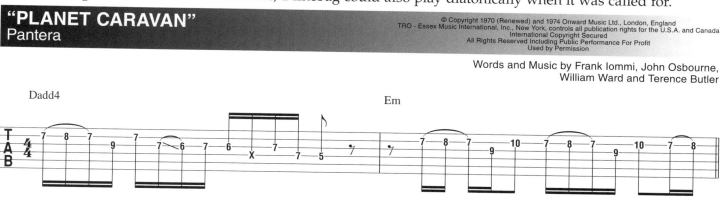

Be sure to practice these licks in other keys and areas of the fretboard. And try to work them into your own solos. Before you know it, your neighbors will be banging their heads rather than banging on your door!

MODERN METAL GUITAR

Contrary to what you may have heard, metal is still alive and well. Bands like Lamb of God, System of a Down, Slipknot, Trivium, Mastodon, and many others are picking up where the older metal bands have left off. In this lesson, we're going to study the techniques and elements behind modern metal—from riffs to lead lines and beyond—and help carry the metal torch into the next generation.

Tuning

Why do metal guitars sound so brutally evil, you may ask? Well, one big reason is because the strings are tuned way down. One of the more common tunings is Drop D tuning, down one full step. We'll check out this tuning and some variations on it. Play each string and match your string pitches to the DVD.

C–G–C–F–A–D

 If your strings are buzzing against the frets, you may want to try heavier string gauges to accommodate the slack tuning. You'll probably need to adjust your guitar to accommodate the heavier strings. This is called a "setup" and is a basic job that any competent guitar tech can do (or that you can learn to do yourself).

"Chop Suey!" by System of a Down uses this tuning.

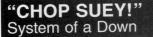

Words and Music by Daron Malakian
and Serj Tankian

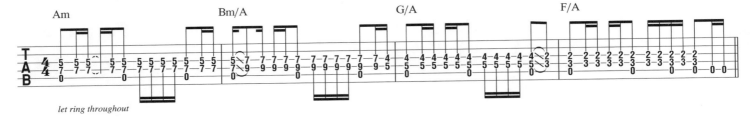

On "Wait and Bleed," Slipknot uses the same tuning a half step lower. This gives us, low to high, B–F♯–B–E–G♯–C♯.

Words and Music by M. Shawn Crahan, Paul Gray,
Nathan Jordison and Corey Taylor

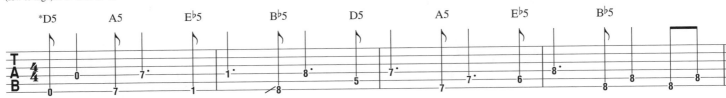

"Black" by Sevendust uses this tuning as well, only a half step higher: D♭–A♭–D♭–G♭–B♭–E♭.

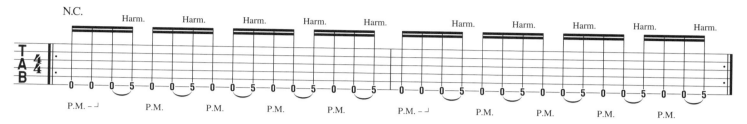

Written by Sevendust

Tone

Perhaps the most obvious component of the metal guitar sound is distortion. You can achieve this with distortion pedals and most amplifiers. Some favorite amps are the Mesa Boogie Dual Rectifier and the Peavey 6505 (formerly known as the 5150).

Many metal guitarists will also use an equalizer on their tone to scoop out the midrange so the highs and lows are boosted. This EQ setting was popularized by Metallica and resembles a "V" shape on a graphic EQ. It gives a tight, thick sound with less of the midrange blare.

Modern Metal Rhythm Guitar

Let's revisit *palm muting*, which we covered earlier in the Metal Rhythm Guitar lesson. It's such an important part of the style that if you skipped ahead to this section, you'll want to carefully pay attention here. To palm mute, use the heel of your picking hand palm and let it rest on the strings just above the bridge. The farther away from the bridge you lay your palm, the more muted the sound becomes.

Here's a basic palm-muted riff. Lift your palm up slightly for the non-muted chords. The dropped tuning makes it possible to play one-finger power chords.

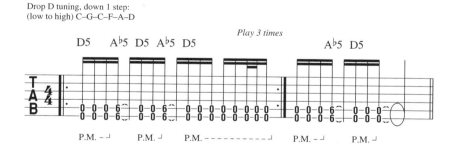

Watch the DVD and check out how the palm of the picking hand is lifted for each non-muted chord.

Here's another one. This one is palm muted throughout. You can use just your first finger of the fretting hand to get to all the notes.

Drop D tuning, down 1 step:
(low to high) C–G–C–F–A–D

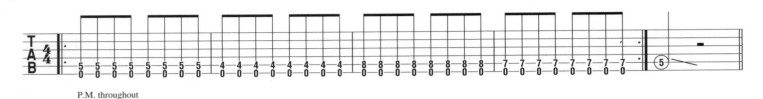

P.M. throughout

Check out the palm muting in the bridge of "Chop Suey!"

"CHOP SUEY!"
System of a Down

Words and Music by Daron Malakian
and Serj Tankian

Drop D tuning, down 1 step:
(low to high) C-G-C-F-A-D

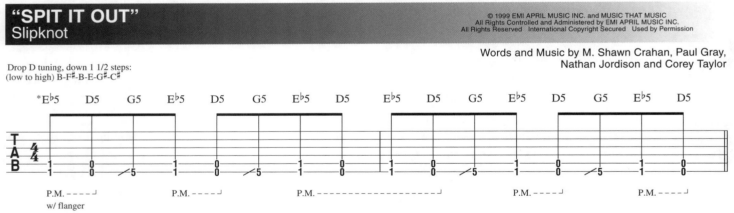

P.M.

The intro to Slipknot's "Spit It Out" also makes use of palm muting.

"SPIT IT OUT"
Slipknot

Words and Music by M. Shawn Crahan, Paul Gray,
Nathan Jordison and Corey Taylor

Drop D tuning, down 1 1/2 steps:
(low to high) B-F#-B-E-G#-C#

*E♭5   D5   G5   E♭5   D5   G5   E♭5   D5   E♭5   D5   G5   E♭5   D5   G5   E♭5   D5

```
T  4
A  4  1    0       1    0       1    0    1    0       1    0       1    0    1    0
B  4  1    0   5   1    0   5   1    0   1    0   5   1    0   5   1    0
```

P.M. ----⌐   P.M. ----⌐   P.M. --------------⌐   P.M. ----⌐   P.M. ----⌐
w/ flanger

*Chord symbols reflect basic harmony.

Alternate Picking

Another element of metal guitar is the use of *alternate picking,* or down-and-up picking. Combine this with palm muting, and you've got pretty much all you need to start writing your own riffs. Here are several that focus on alternate picking.

For this one, you can also use a one-finger approach in your fretting hand.

Drop D tuning, down 1 step:
(low to high) C–G–C–F–A–D

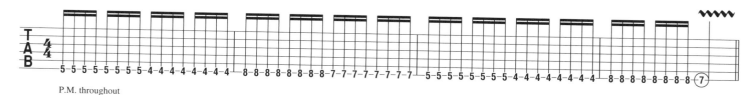

P.M. throughout

 Here's one without palm muting. It's a bit of a finger twister!

Drop D tuning, down 1 step:
(low to high) C–G–C–F–A–D

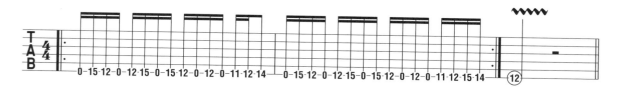

 When you alternate pick, keep yourself relaxed and try to minimize your hand movement. Pick from the wrist and not the arm. Watch the DVD to see what we mean.

Alternate pick through this one and accent the notes with the accent mark (>).

"HEY MAN NICE SHOT"
Filter

Words and Music by
Richard Patrick

Drop D tuning:
(low to high) D-A-D-G-B-E

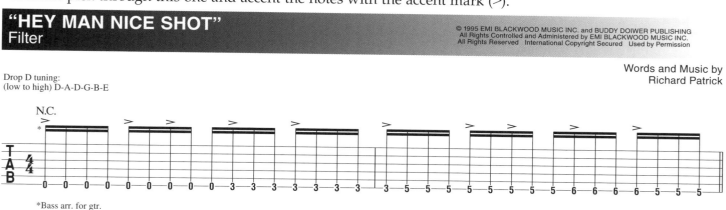

*Bass arr. for gtr.

Advanced Rhythms

Playing tight rhythm is crucial in a metal guitar band. Listen to bands like Lamb of God and Mastodon, and you'll hear how cool it sounds when the guitars and drums lock in together for fast, complex rhythms. To make it work though, you have to make sure everyone is together rhythmically; otherwise, it will sound like a big mess.

Let's check out some interesting rhythms to work on. Tip: Don't hold the tied note too long and keep the rhythms tight and crisp.

Drop D tuning, down 1 step:
(low to high) C–G–C–F–A–D

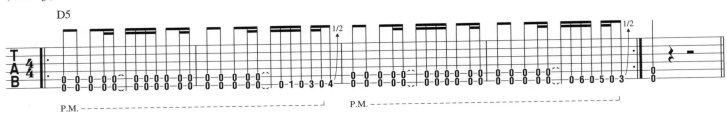

 Here's a fun one. The rhythms are tricky, so you should definitely check out the DVD first to make sure you're doing it right. There's a slow demo as well.

Drop D tuning, down 1 step:
(low to high) C–G–C–F–A–D

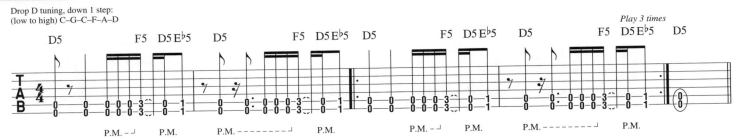

 The thirty-second notes in the latter half of this next riff should sound like a demon tip-toeing through your backyard.

Drop D tuning, down 1 step:
(low to high) C–G–C–F–A–D

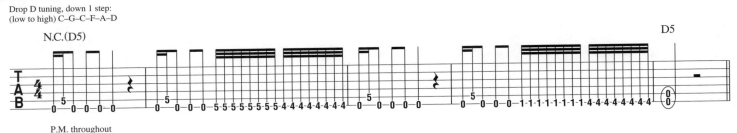

 Here's another one. Use hammer-ons and pull-offs for the first part of the lick (this is indicated by the slur, which is the curvy line under the numbers in the tab).

Drop D tuning, down 1 step:
(low to high) C–G–C–F–A–D

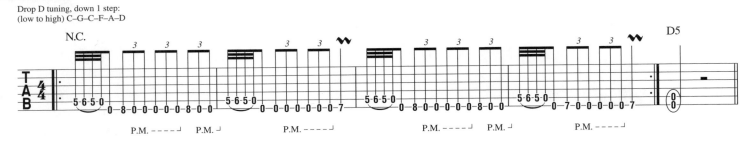

The chorus of 311's "Come Original" makes use of some advanced rhythms.

Music by Nicholas Hexum and Aaron Wills
Lyrics by Nicholas Hexum and Doug Martinez

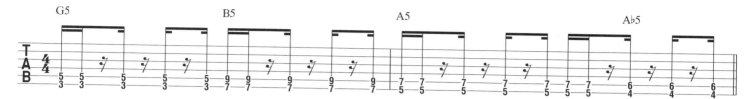

Modern Metal Lead Guitar

There are a lot of different approaches you can take to playing lead in a metal song. Some bands prefer to include the traditional guitar solo, which is usually more expressive and technically challenging. Others use harmonized lead lines to create an instrumental theme or melody. And still others leave out the lead playing entirely, using higher-pitched guitar lines to enhance the rhythm parts. Let's take a look at all of these components, and you can decide what works best for you.

Octave Lines

Modern metal bands often use octave lines to thicken a melodic line or rhythm part. The basic octave shape somewhat resembles a power chord, in that it's a two-note shape with one fret between the two notes. However, while the two notes of a power chord are played on adjacent strings, the octave shape has one string between the two fingers. The string in between is not played and muted with the fretting hand.

 This one is rooted on the fifth string. The index finger should touch the fourth string to keep it from ringing when strumming through the three strings. You only want to hear the two octave notes. Otherwise it could get messy sounding.

 When an octave shape is rooted on the fourth string, the shape changes slightly because of the B string. Instead of having one fret in between, now there are two frets in between. You might want to use your pinky, as there is a bigger stretch involved.

 The same thing occurs with an octave shape rooted on the third string. You'll have to stretch the pinky.

 In Drop D tuning, here's how the shape would look rooted on the sixth string. The sixth and fourth strings are the same pitch, so the two notes are on the same fret:

And here's a typical octave line. If you're comfortable moving your power chords around, this shouldn't be too much harder.

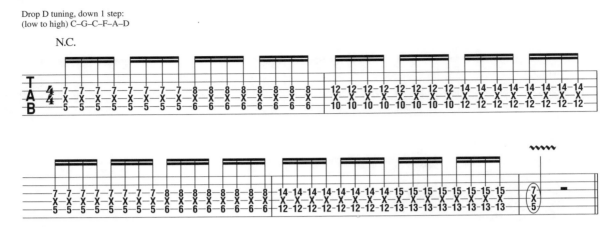

The guitar solo from System of a Down's "Spiders" uses octaves to create a roller coaster effect.

"SPIDERS"
System of a Down

Words and Music by Daron Malakian, Serj Tankian,
Shavo Odadjian and John Dolmayan

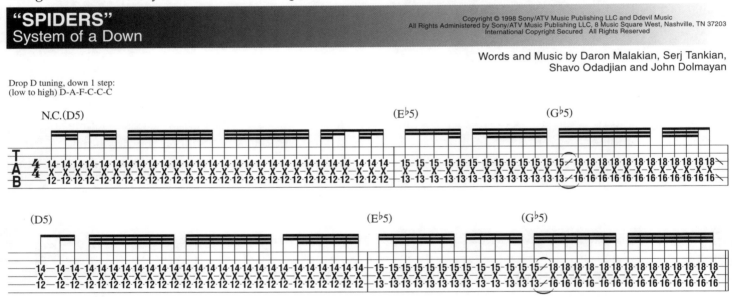

In "Wait and Bleed," Slipknot feels the hate and lets us know with brutal octaves that sound like buzzing bees.

"WAIT AND BLEED"
Slipknot

Words and Music by M. Shawn Crahan, Paul Gray,
Nathan Jordison and Corey Taylor

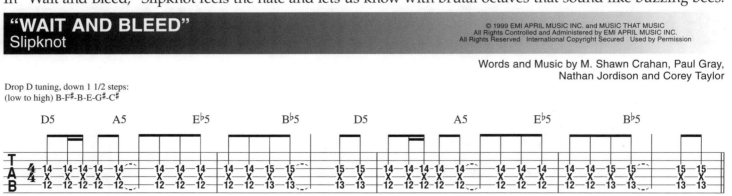

Effects

A lot of metal players will add effects to their lead lines to give them a different texture, make them stand out from the rest of the band, and inspire nightmares. Some common effects are wah-wah, chorus, delay, Whammy pedals, and envelope filters.

Here's a cool trick: Take a wah pedal and use it on the octave line we just played. Start with the pedal all the way back and very gradually push down as you play the example. Have your toe all the way down during the last measure. Sinister, eh?

Tremolo Picking

Let's talk about an idea that's similar to the octave line called *tremolo picking*. This is basically alternate picking as fast as you can. You can take single-note lines and move them around on one string to create moving lines. You dictate the rhythm with your fret hand instead of your pick hand. The pick hand just keeps alternate picking very fast while you move notes around on one string. The key is to not let your picking hand tire out and get sluggish.

Drop D tuning, down 1 step:
(low to high) C–G–C–F–A–D

Tune your guitar A–A–D–G–B–E, low-to-high, to play the tremolo-picked octaves in Filter's "Welcome to the Fold." See how important de-tuning is for modern metal?

"WELCOME TO THE FOLD"
Filter

Words and Music by
Richard Patrick

Drop A tuning:
(low to high) A–A-D-G-B-E

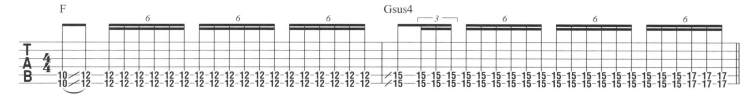

Harmonized Lead Lines

Another option you'll hear used often by modern metal bands is harmonized lead lines. This is probably an off-shoot of the Iron Maiden influence, albeit with a modern twist. Bands like Avenged Sevenfold and Atreyu will double up certain parts of the song, both rhythm and lead, with harmonized lines. Let's check out an example.

Here's the melody line. It's based on a neo-classical sounding D minor arpeggio riff followed by an E arpeggio riff.

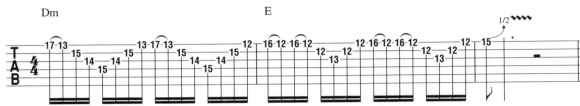

 And here's the harmony line, which is based on another shape of the D minor and E arpeggios.

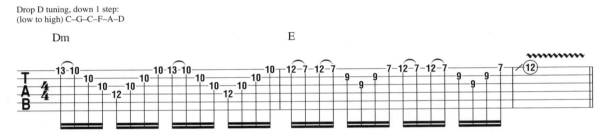

 On the DVD, check out the melody along with a playback of the harmony. Sweet!

This riff, from 311's "Come Original," starts with two guitars playing octaves and two more guitars coming in later to add harmony. If you can't round up three other guitarists, you can use a looping pedal to record the other parts into and play against.

"COME ORIGINAL"
311

Music by Nicholas Hexum and Aaron Wills
Lyrics by Nicholas Hexum and Doug Martinez

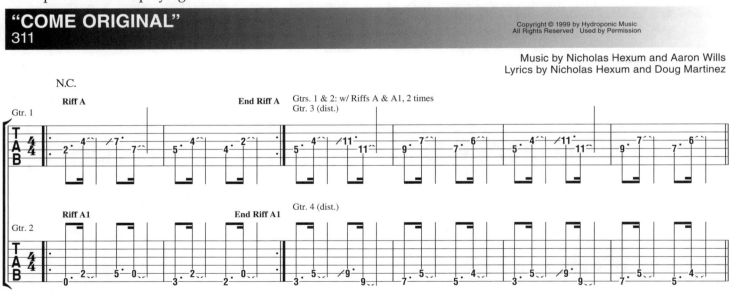

Here are more harmonized octaves, as used in Coal Chamber's "Tyler's Song."

"TYLER'S SONG"
Coal Chamber

**Words and Music by Bradley Fafara, Mike Cox,
Rayna Foss and Miguel Rascon**

Tune down as follows:
(low to high) B-E-A-D-G-B

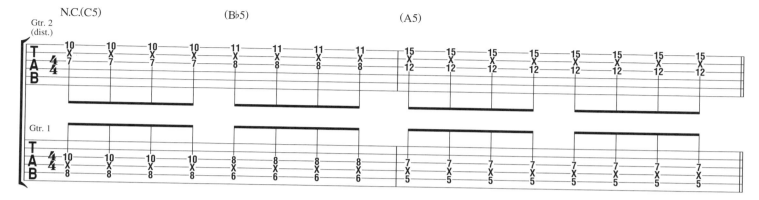

JAMES HETFIELD STYLE

Metallica's James Hetfield composed some of the greatest metal riffs of all time—from "Seek and Destroy" to "Master of Puppets" to "Enter Sandman" and beyond. While Hetfield had a knack for writing the heaviest riffs, his tool box consisted of all the essentials that we've learned—especially power chords and palm muting. Let's check out how Hetfield used these devices and learn some killer riffs in the process.

Tone

The first thing you're going to need to get that Hetfield sound is some serious distortion. James favored amp distortion (mainly Mesa Boogie) over pedals and usually equalized his tone to achieve a thick bottom end, piercing high end, and very little midrange. Remember the "V" shape we talked about on page 22? That's it—highs, lows, and no mids. Got it?

Punishing Power Chords

The basic component of all metal guitar is the *power chord*, and no doubt Hetfield fueled the Metallica machine with of a steady diet of power chords. Again, power chords contain only roots and 5ths (they are also called "5" chords because of that). James favors the two-note variety for easy access and speed.

As you learned earlier, you can move this two-note power chord shape anywhere on the fretboard on the bottom four strings. If you skipped directly to this section, take a few minutes to watch the DVD and first try the B♭5 chord.

Then the E5 on the fifth string:

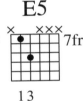

Now try putting the power chords in action. You can move these suckers all over the place. Here, the Devil's tritone adds to the evil!

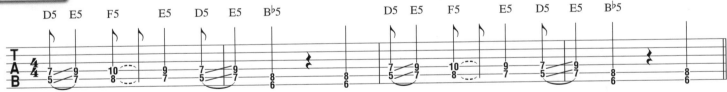

"Am I Evil?" uses a lot those power chords you just played!

"AM I EVIL?"
Metallica

Words and Music by Sean Harris
and Brian Tatler

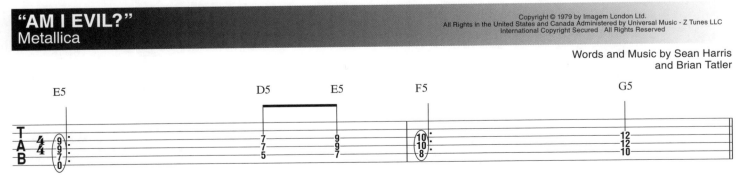

Palm Muting and Downstroking

Another integral part of Hetfield's rhythm guitar style is the use of *palm muting*. This will give you that classic Metallica chugging sound, so it's really important that you get this technique down cold. The farther you move your palm away from the bridge, the more muted and percussive the sound gets.

In addition to palm muting in his riffs, another thing Hetfield often does is use all *downstrokes* with his picking hand, even with the fast stuff. This gives a machine-gun-like attack to the sound, adding some much-needed brutality to the proceedings. This can be pretty hard at first, and it may take some time to get close to Hetfield's level of endurance. If it's super, super fast, then he'll use alternate picking, or down-and-up picking strokes.

Here's the power-chord riff from before but now with an added palm-muted chug on the low E string in between the chords. You'll have to lift your palm slightly off the strings every time you hit a chord and lay it back down for the palm-muted E string. It's also important that you not rush the slid power chords. This may take some coordination to get the rhythmic feel right, and if you don't get it right away, try it slowly at first.

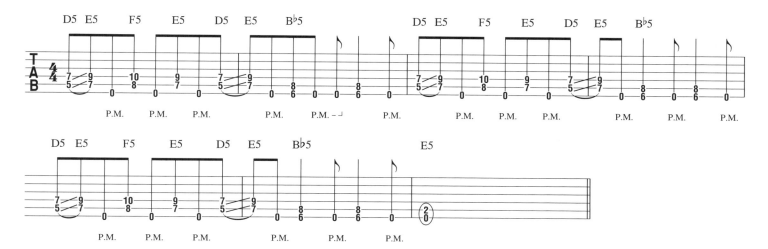

After you get the coordination, try the riff faster. Study the movement of the pick hand by watching the DVD. The trick is that you can gain more downstroking speed by allowing the picking motion to come from the wrist and not the arm.

You can break up the repetition a bit by adding a riff change here. Hetfield often combined many different riffs with contrasting rhythms and techniques in his compositions to create epic headbanging masterpieces. Here, we'll take the first riff and add some tritone mayhem at the end.

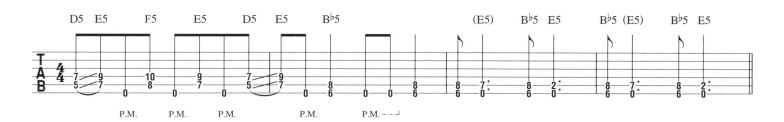

Palm Muting Power Chords

You can also get a nice chunky sound if you palm mute your power chords like in this riff, inspired by "For Whom the Bell Tolls." Make sure that, in addition to muting both notes of the chord, your pick also hits both notes of the chord. Sometimes when people first learn power chords, even if they finger the chord right, they unintentionally only pick one out of two strings, and the chord ends up sounding kind of limp.

 This riff starts on the "and" of beat 4, so listen carefully to get the timing right.

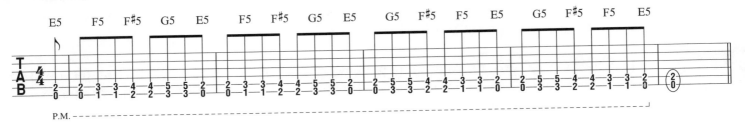

 You can break things up by alternating between those chords you just played and a palm-muted open low E string. This lick is reminiscent of "The Thing That Should Not Be."

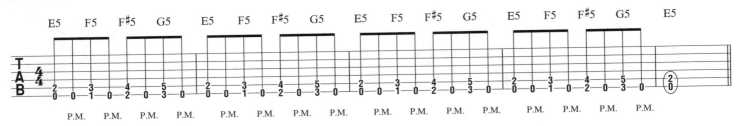

Towards the end of "Breadfan," chunky, muted E power chords played in a unison rhythm with the band help round out the song. There's no mute on the last chord, so lift up that palm.

"BREADFAN"
Metallica

Words and Music by Anthony Bourge,
John Burke Shelley and Raymond Phillips

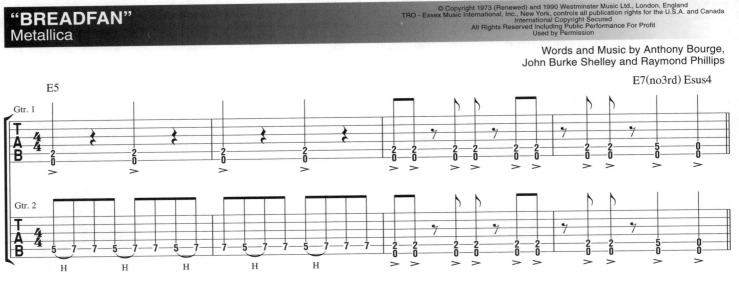

Alternate Picking

When things got *really* fast, Hetfield also used a lot of alternate picking on the low strings in his riffs. To maintain speed and accuracy, the picking motion should come from the wrist. First try it out on just the low E string with the obligatory palm mute. If you do it right, it should sound like a machine gun.

Watch the DVD and notice how minimal the wrist movement is. Not a whole lot of motion is needed to make this happen.

 Here's a riff inspired by "Whiplash." While there's very little activity in the left hand, the right hand really takes a whipping here.

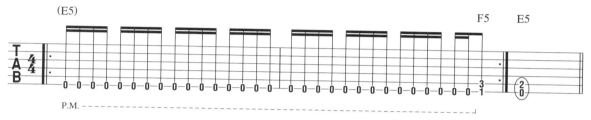

 Mr. Hetfield would also break up this alternate picking style into more complex rhythms. Let's add some sixteenth-note alternate picking to the power-chord riff we played earlier. Just by adding the sixteenths, the riff becomes an entirely different beast.

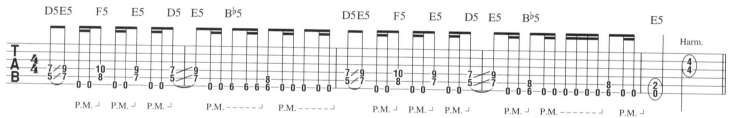

 You can create a galloping effect by playing palm-muted triplets, as in "The Four Horsemen." Let the momentum of the last triplet downstroke carry the pick into the fifth-string power chord. It should feel pretty natural, but it might also be helpful to watch the slow version on the DVD.

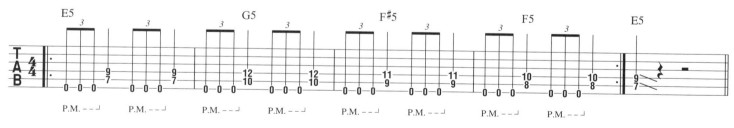

Try the open E triplets in "Am I Evil?" Be sure to keep the rhythms tight.

"AM I EVIL?"
Metallica

Words and Music by Sean Harris
and Brian Tatler

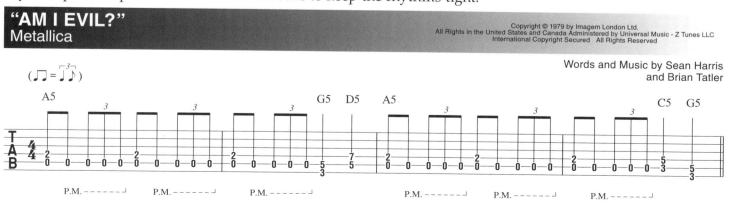

Single-Note Riffs

Of course there are many great single-note Metallica-type riffs to explore as well. Here's one that sounds kind of like "No Remorse" mixed with "Master of Puppets." Use all downstrokes and palm mute the low E-string notes. If you want to "cheat," you can just use one finger to play all the fretted notes; just don't let your guitar teacher see you doing that!

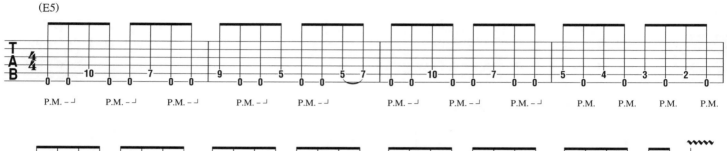

Here's one that sounds more like something from nineties Metallica, with a definite Black Sabbath influence. It's got a catchy vibe that's more bluesy than evil. Notice that there's a triplet or *swing* feel on the eighth notes, so play the first eighth of each eighth-note group longer than the second eighth.

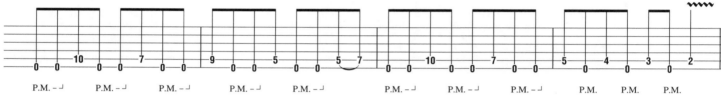

Hetfield also uses a lot of cool techniques in his riffs including slurs, slides, and pull-offs to open strings. This next lick packs all these tricks into a killer package.

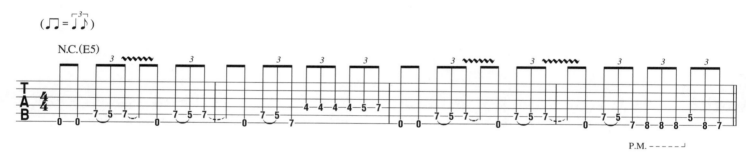

Here's Metallica's take on "Stone Cold Crazy."

"STONE COLD CRAZY"
Metallica

Words and Music by Freddie Mercury, Brian May,
Roger Taylor and John Deacon

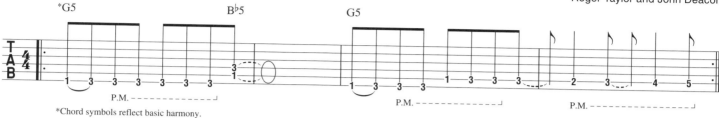

*Chord symbols reflect basic harmony.

Check out the bluesy riff from "Breadfan" that comes right after Kirk Hammet's blistering solo. This is set against a half-time feel.

"BREADFAN"
Metallica

Words and Music by Anthony Bourge,
John Burke Shelley and Raymond Phillips

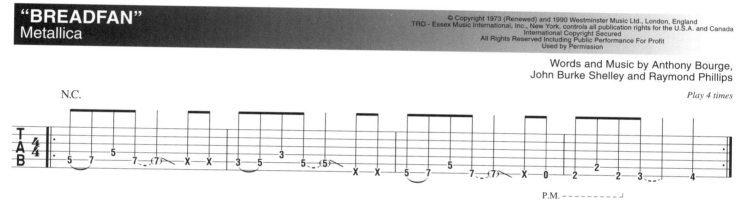

Clean Riffs

There are many great Hetfield riffs that *aren't* distorted as well. Think of the classic Metallica tunes, and almost all of them have some sort of great arpeggio-type clean riff: "Fade to Black," "Sanitarium," and "One," just to name a few. If you saw the Metallic documentary *Some Kind of Monster*, then you know that the bad boys of Metallica can hurt too, and what better way to share your pain than with clean-toned arpeggios?

An *arpeggio* is a chord played one note at a time. This first one uses some of the chord shapes that James uses frequently in his clean riffs. These chords are "spiced-up" versions of common chords, with ringing open strings added to wring out the tears.

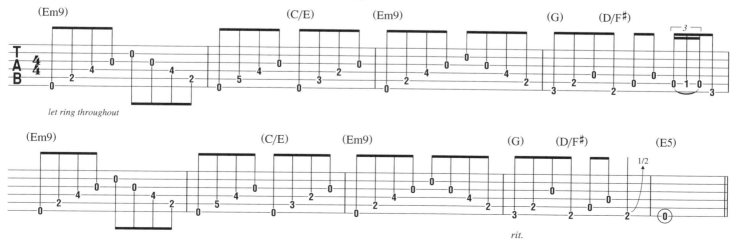

Here's another one that harkens back to "…And Justice for All." Notice how very simple shapes and patterns are often used to make the riffs relatively easy to play, yet they still sound really cool. Remember, just because something is easy doesn't mean it's bad; conversely, just because something is hard doesn't mean it's good.

 You might want to experiment with moving around two-string shapes against a low open string; maybe you'll create the next metal hit.

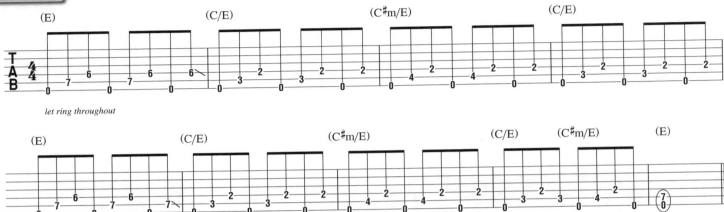

 Here's one more arpeggio riff that sounds a bit like a cross between the intros to "Enter Sandman" and "Call of Ktulu." There's nothing like adding a tritone to rain on a parade already laden with darkness!

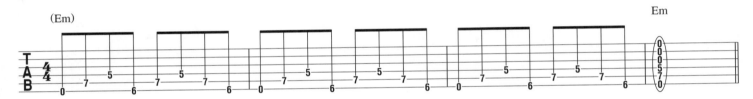

Hetfield creates an eerie haunting vibe in the interlude to "Breadfan" by mixing up arppegiatted E minor and D minor barre chord shapes against a ringing, open high E string.

"BREADFAN" INTERLUDE
Metallica

Words and Music by Anthony Bourge,
John Burke Shelley and Raymond Phillips

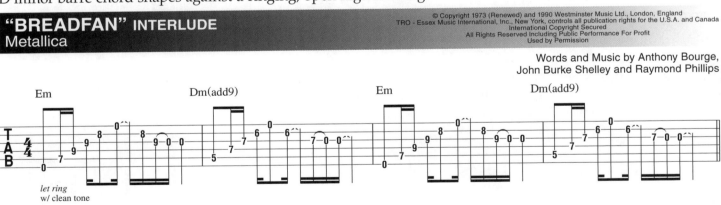

RANDY RHOADS STYLE

Randy Rhoads was undeniably one of the most influential heavy metal guitarists ever. With his original classically-inspired sound, he revitalized the metal genre and paved the way for the shredding movement that followed.

Let's take a look at the key elements of the Rhoads style and learn what made him such a unique and memorable talent in the guitar world.

Rhythm Playing

Randy was a riff-*meister*, and his are some of the most memorable in all of metal. Let's take a look at some of his favorite tools for playing rhythm parts.

Pedal Tones

We checked out pedal tones in the metal rhythm lesson, and they were among Randy's favorite devices. Again, a pedal tone is basically a repeated bass note under a series of changing chords. In the heavy metal style, this usually means palm muting a low note and interjecting some chord jabs above. This is one of the most fundamental elements of metal, and Ozzy's "Crazy Train" and "I Don't Know" are excellent examples of this.

Here's an example of this classic device in the very common key of A minor.

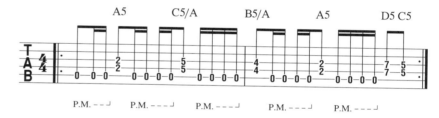

In this example, the open A string is our pedal tone, and we're playing two-note power chords above it on strings 4 and 3. Use alternate picking for the open-string notes. Note that every time you strike a chord, you'll use a downstroke.

Also be sure to mute the low A string for a more percussive sound and then release the palm mute for the power chords.

All aboard!

"CRAZY TRAIN"
Ozzy Osbourne

Words and Music by Ozzy Osbourne,
Randy Rhoads and Bob Daisley

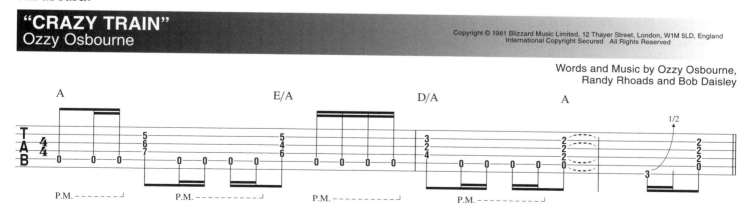

Arpeggiation

A lot of times, Randy would arpeggiate chords as a form of contrast—in a bridge to a song, maybe, or in a ballad, and with a cleaner tone. You hear this approach in "Goodbye to Romance" and in the bridge to "I Don't Know."

He usually stuck to mostly chords tones but would add some decorations every now and then with scalar runs, double-stop figures, or passing tones. A basic rule with embellishments is to not overdo them.

 Here's an example of this style:

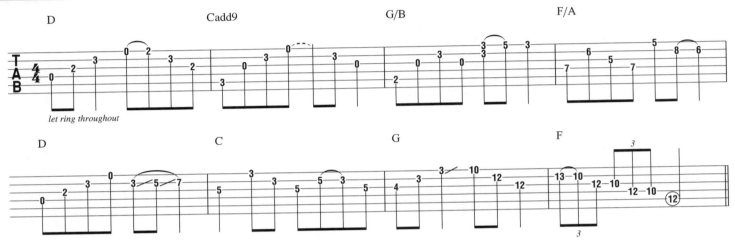

In that example, we're just playing through the chord tones or adding little embellishments with other scale tones. Most of this progression has a D Mixolydian sound, so that's the scale most of the embellishments come from. But the F chord at the end of the progression is borrowed from the parallel D *minor*, so on that chord we draw from the D minor scale, or, more specifically in this case, D minor pentatonic.

A good way to start coming up with embellishments is to take a common chord shape and find notes that are both in the same key and also physically nearby. For example, the D chord in that last example added the open high E string in addition to the second-fret F♯ that is in the D chord. Other notes on the high E string that are nearby the D chord's F♯ note could be the third-fret G, which would create a suspended 4th sound against the D, and the 5th fret A, which is a chord tone (the 5th).

Check out Randy's work in the verse and chorus of "Goodbye to Romance" to see arpeggiation and melodic fills used for a rhythm guitar part.

"GOODBYE TO ROMANCE" VERSE Ozzy Osbourne	

Words and Music by John Osbourne,
Robert Daisley and Randy Rhoads

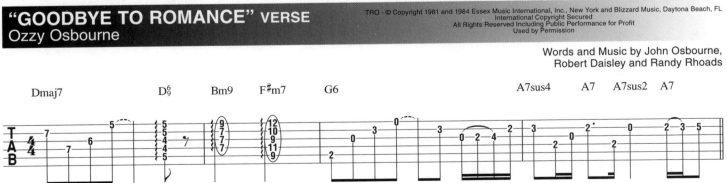

"GOODBYE TO ROMANCE" CHORUS
Ozzy Osbourne

Words and Music by John Osbourne,
Robert Daisley and Randy Rhoads

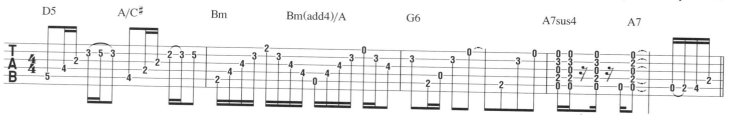

Fills

Another thing Randy was a master of was adding fills into his rock riffs. There was rarely a dead space in a Randy Rhoads track, yet it never sounded like overkill. Let's look at some of his favorite types of fills.

Pinch Harmonics

One of the simplest tricks is a well-placed *pinch harmonic*. It's a good way to really grab the listener's ear.

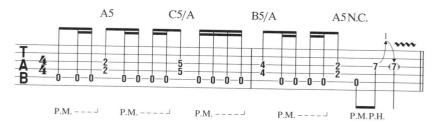

To produce a pinch harmonic, choke up on the pick a bit and have your thumb brush the string at the same time the pick does. It'll take a bit of practice, and it might be a while before you even get one to pop out, but you'll eventually get it down and intuitively know how to angle your thumb and pick.

In the interlude to "Suicide Solution," Randy makes great use of a pinch harmonic.

"SUICIDE SOLUTION"
Ozzy Osbourne

Words and Music by John Osbourne,
Robert Daisley and Randy Rhoads

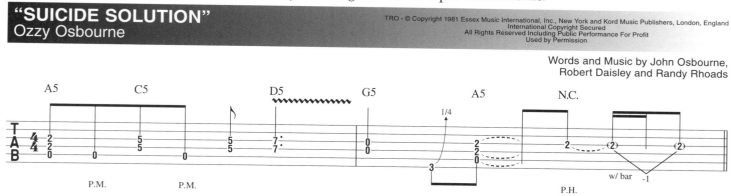

Natural Harmonics

Randy also made use of *natural harmonics* in his fills. The ones on the fifth and seventh fret were the most common, but you can also experiment with other locations like the twelfth fret. He'd usually add a dip with the bar or bend the neck to make them stick out a bit more.

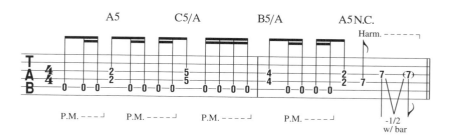

Caution: extreme bending could damage the guitar neck!

Randy strikes some seventh-fret harmonics, and then gives it a whammy dive in the chorus of "Crazy Train."

"CRAZY TRAIN"
Ozzy Osbourne

Words and Music by Ozzy Osbourne,
Randy Rhoads and Bob Daisley

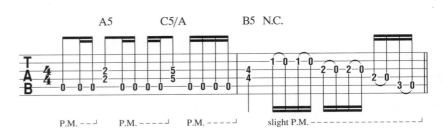

Open-String Pull-Offs

Another favorite fill of Randy's was cascading down the Am chord form with pull-offs to the open strings. He did this all the time.

You'll need to use some left-hand muting to make sure you're not allowing the open strings to ring out. Otherwise it could turn to mush, especially if you've got a lot of gain on.

Here are two examples of Randy using open-string pull-offs from "I Don't know." The first one goes from the second string down to the fifth string, while the second one stays on only one string, moving down from the fifth fret to the second fret.

"I DON'T KNOW" #1
Ozzy Osbourne

Words and Music by Ozzy Osbourne,
Randy Rhoads and Bob Daisley

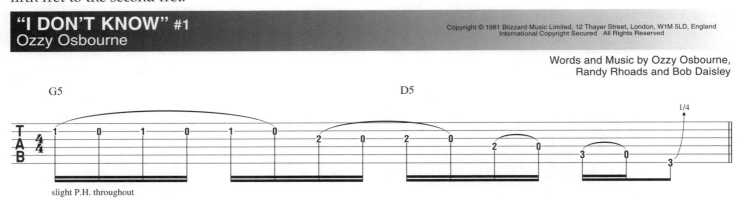

"I DON'T KNOW" #2
Ozzy Osbourne

Words and Music by Ozzy Osbourne,
Randy Rhoads and Bob Daisley

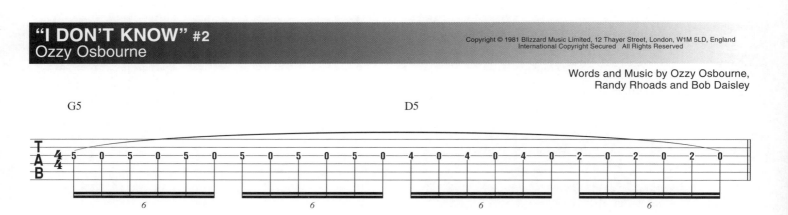

Double Stops

Though not often used in metal, Randy would occasionally whip out some double-stop 3rds during a fill. This was no-doubt influenced by his classical guitar studies.

In "Mr. Crowley," Randy uses double-stop 3rds as a fill.

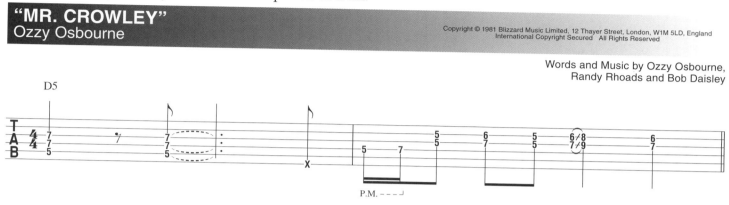

Words and Music by Ozzy Osbourne,
Randy Rhoads and Bob Daisley

The thing with fills is that you want to be careful not to overdo it; just exercise good taste here. You also have to make sure that when you finish the fill you can get back to the riff you're playing perfectly in time; otherwise, it sounds amateur-ish.

Solos

When it came to solos, Randy was one of the greatest of all time. His leads were exciting, melodic, virtuosic, and very memorable. They usually contained both flash and melody and were constructed with a logical sense of direction and purpose. He, along with Eddie Van Halen and Yngwie Malmsteen, raised the bar for guitar solos and changed its direction from a blues-based language to the shred craze of the eighties.

Repetetive Licks

One of Randy's favorite solo devices was the fast, repetitive lick, usually from a minor pentatonic scale. You can hear these types of licks in "Flying High Again," "Mr. Crowley," and "Crazy Train," to name a few.

Here are some examples in D minor. The trick here is to not hang on to that bent note too long; just keep the lick moving.

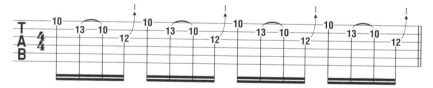

This one's a little quicker, but the pull-offs help with the speed.

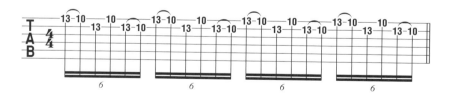

This one sounds good with a little palm muting.

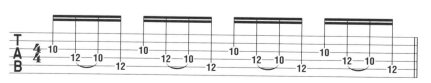

P.M. throughout

Here's a cool, repetitive tapping lick from "Crazy Train."

"CRAZY TRAIN"
Ozzy Osbourne

Words and Music by Ozzy Osbourne,
Randy Rhoads and Bob Daisley

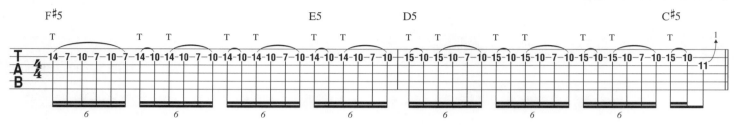

And here's a bluesy, repeating F# minor pentatonic lick from "Flying High Again."

"FLYING HIGH AGAIN"
Ozzy Osbourne

Words and Music by Ozzy Osbourne, Randy Rhoads,
Bob Daisley and Lee Kerslake

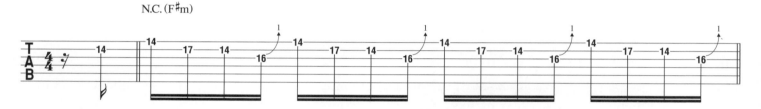

Sequences

Randy was really influenced by classical music, and this can be heard in his use of sequences. Sometimes these were flashy pentatonic runs, as in "Mr. Crowley."

This is a fairly common and very useful sequence and should be added to your bag of licks.

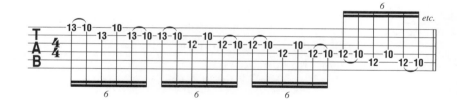

Sometimes Randy played more melodic diatonic phrases as in "Goodbye to Romance." This lick should be played with strict alternate picking.

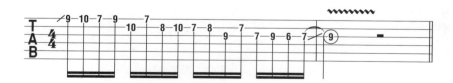

The diminished 7th arpeggio sequence is a signature Randy Rhoads lick. He would stick it into his leads sometimes, and it always added a sense of drama. You can hear this in "Steal Away the Night" and the live version of "Suicide Solution," during the cadenza.

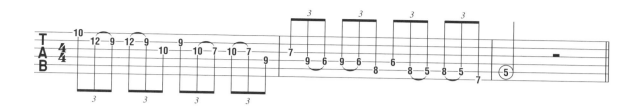

Learn this classical-inspired arpeggio sequence from "Mr. Crowley," and your friends will be blown away.

"MR. CROWLEY"
Ozzy Osbourne

Words and Music by Ozzy Osbourne,
Randy Rhoads and Bob Daisley

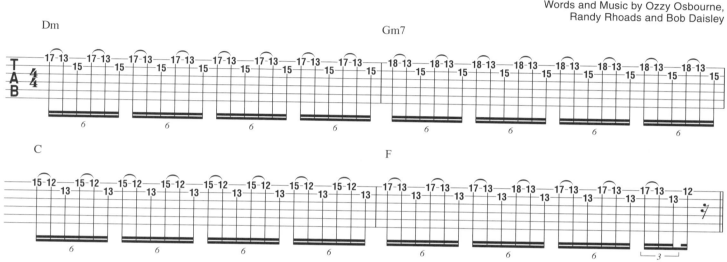

Natural Minor/Blues Hybrid Scale

One of Randy's trademark sounds was his mixture of the natural minor and blues scales. This is one of the elements that distinguished Randy from his blues-based only peers. Listen to "I Don't Know" and "Crazy Train" for classic examples of this.

In the key of A minor, the scale would look like this in the familiar fifth position form:

Here's a typical Rhoads lick with this form. Try and visualize the pentatonic shape, keeping it as a reference, even as you play the natural minor based parts of the lick.

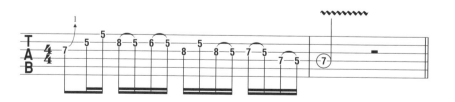

Here's a great A natural minor/blues combo lick from "I Don't Know."

"I DON'T KNOW"
Ozzy Osbourne

Words and Music by Ozzy Osbourne,
Randy Rhoads and Bob Daisley

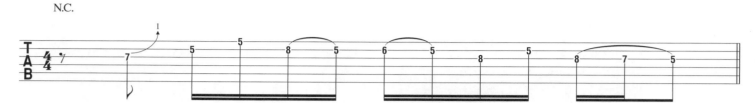

Moving Licks Chromatically

Another classic Rhoads device is to take a short lick and move it chromatically up or down. This creates an "outside" effect and can make you think you're losing your mind and/or that your head's gonna explode. He used this technique for some fills on "Crazy Train" and in the solos of "I Don't Know" and "Suicide Solution," among others.

Here's an example in A minor. This lick is sixteenth-note based but grouped in three-note fragments, so a cool "against-the-time" vibe is created.

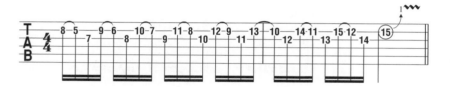

This lick, from the "Crazy Train" solo, takes a pentatonic bending shape and moves it up fret-by-fret from the fourteenth fret F# to the eighteenth fret.

"CRAZY TRAIN"
Ozzy Osbourne

Words and Music by Ozzy Osbourne,
Randy Rhoads and Bob Daisley

Be sure to add palm muting to this descending chromatic lick from "I Don't Know."

"I DON'T KNOW"
Ozzy Osbourne

Words and Music by Ozzy Osbourne,
Randy Rhoads and Bob Daisley

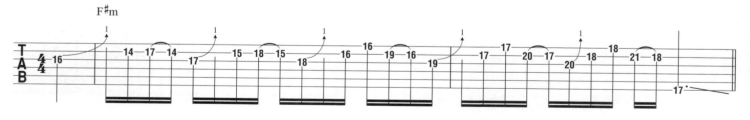

Rhythm Tab Legend

Rhythm Tab is a form of notation that adds rhythmic values to the traditional tab staff.

TABLATURE graphically represents the guitar fingerboard. Each horizontal line represents a string, and each number represents a fret. Rhythmic values are shown using ovals, stems, and dots.

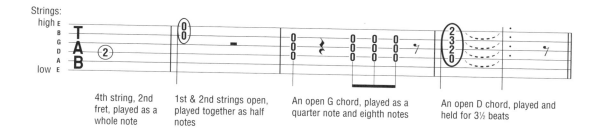

4th string, 2nd fret, played as a whole note

1st & 2nd strings open, played together as half notes

An open G chord, played as a quarter note and eighth notes

An open D chord, played and held for 3½ beats

Definitions for Special Guitar Notation

HALF-STEP BEND: Strike the note and bend up 1/2 step.

WHOLE-STEP BEND: Strike the note and bend up one step.

GRACE NOTE BEND: Strike the note and immediately bend up as indicated.

SLIGHT (MICROTONE) BEND: Strike the note and bend up 1/4 step.

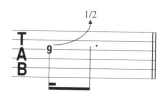

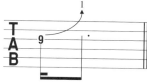

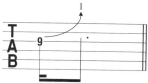

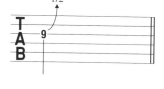

BEND AND RELEASE: Strike the note and bend up as indicated, then release back to the original note. Only the first note is struck.

PRE-BEND: Bend the note as indicated, then strike it.

PRE-BEND AND RELEASE: Bend the note as indicated. Strike it and release the bend back to the original note.

UNISON BEND: Strike the two notes simultaneously and bend the lower note up to the pitch of the higher.

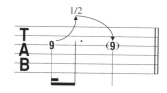

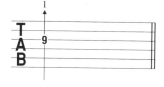

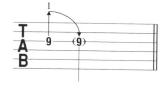

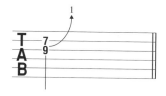

HOLD BEND: While sustaining bent note, strike note on different string.

VIBRATO: The string is vibrated by rapidly bending and releasing the note with the fretting hand.

WIDE VIBRATO: The pitch is varied to a greater degree by vibrating with the fretting hand.

HAMMER-ON: Strike the first (lower) note with one finger, then sound the higher note (on the same string) with another finger by fretting it without picking.

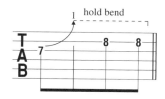

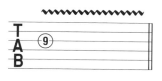

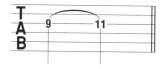

PULL-OFF: Place both fingers on the notes to be sounded. Strike the first note and without picking, pull the finger off to sound the second (lower) note.

HAMMER FROM NOWHERE: Sound note(s) by hammering with fret hand finger only.

GRACE NOTE SLUR: Strike the note and immediately hammer-on (or pull-off) as indicated.

GRACE NOTE SLUR (CLUSTER): Strike the notes and immediately hammer-on (or pull-off) as indicated.

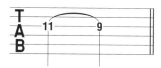

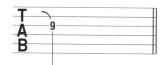

LEGATO SLIDE: Strike the first note and then slide the same fret-hand finger up or down to the second note. The second note is not struck.

SHIFT SLIDE: Same as legato slide, except the second note is struck.

TRILL: Very rapidly alternate between the notes indicated by continuously hammering on and pulling off.

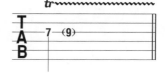

TAPPING: Hammer ("tap") the fret indicated with the pick-hand index or middle finger and pull off to the note fretted by the fret hand.

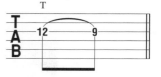

NATURAL HARMONIC: Strike the note while the fret-hand lightly touches the string directly over the fret indicated.

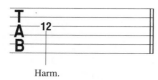

PINCH HARMONIC: The note is fretted normally and a harmonic is produced by adding the edge of the thumb or the tip of the index finger of the pick hand to the normal pick attack.

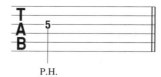

HARP HARMONIC: The note is fretted normally and a harmonic is produced by gently resting the pick hand's index finger directly above the indicated fret (in parentheses) while the pick hand's thumb or pick assists by plucking the appropriate string.

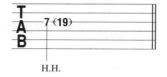

PICK SCRAPE: The edge of the pick is rubbed down (or up) the string, producing a scratchy sound.

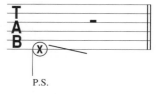

MUFFLED STRINGS: A percussive sound is produced by laying the fret hand across the string(s) without depressing, and striking them with the pick hand.

PALM MUTING: The note is partially muted by the pick hand lightly touching the string(s) just before the bridge.

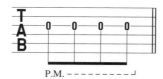

RAKE: Drag the pick across the strings indicated with a single motion.

TREMOLO PICKING: The note is picked as rapidly and continuously as possible.

ARPEGGIATE: Play the notes of the chord indicated by quickly rolling them from bottom to top.

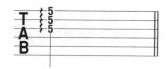

VIBRATO BAR DIVE AND RETURN: The pitch of the note or chord is dropped a specified number of steps (in rhythm), then returned to the original pitch.

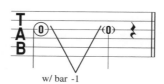

VIBRATO BAR SCOOP: Depress the bar just before striking the note, then quickly release the bar.

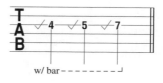

VIBRATO BAR DIP: Strike the note and then immediately drop a specified number of steps, then release back to the original pitch.

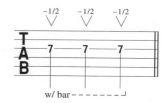

Additional Musical Definitions

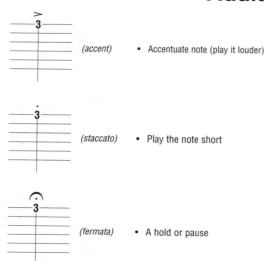

(accent)	• Accentuate note (play it louder)
(staccato)	• Play the note short
(fermata)	• A hold or pause

⊓ • Downstroke

∨ • Upstroke

• Repeat measures between signs

NOTE: Tablature numbers in parentheses are used when:
- The note is sustained, but a new articulation begins (such as a hammer-on, pull-off, slide, or bend), or
- A bend is released.